THE DISAPPEARANCE OF GOD
AND SCIENCE

By the same author:

Freedom of Philosophical Conundrums, The Book Guild, 1995

THE DISAPPEARANCE OF GOD AND SCIENCE

Roland Gibson

The Book Guild Ltd
Sussex, England

This book is sold subject to the condition that it shall not, by way of trade or otherwise, be lent, re-sold, hired out, photocopied or held in any retrieval system or otherwise circulated without the publisher's prior consent in any form of binding or cover other than that in which this is published and without a similar condition including this condition being imposed on the subsequent purchasers.

The Book Guild Ltd.
25 High Street,
Lewes, Sussex

First published 1999
© Roland Gibson 1999

Set in Times
Typesetting by
Acorn Bookwork, Salisbury

Printed in Great Britain by
Bookcraft (Bath) Ltd, Avon

A catalogue record for this book is
available from the British Library

ISBN 1 85776 476 5

CONTENTS

	Preface	vii
	Introduction	1
1	Marxian Value Forms and Group Elements	9
2	Between the Determined and the Undetermined	37
3	The Same Thing Said in Different Words	45
	Appendices	67

PREFACE

This book is addressed to any spiritual casualty of commercial and industrial society – anyone for whom a primitive belief in immortality of the dead disappears into an assertion or statement of 'fact' as something already done. The dead live on as signs and symbols of God and Science, which disappear in individual recognition of one's social existence.

We live in an age of conflicting cultural tendencies which reflect an increasingly complex social and economic context; tendencies manifested at one extreme in a variety of neo-religious cults expressing declining orthodox religious belief, with growing anxiety, and at the other extreme manifested by ever increasing intellectual specialisation in our technological society. In this contrast of the nebulously general versus the narrowly specific there frequently appear newspaper articles on declining standards, stressing the need for a return to traditional norms; also, reports of various God versus Science arguments. So there could appear to be an urgent need for some coherent worldview relating such apparently disparate domains, in order to organise one's experiences in a changing world.

However, such a 'philosophy' already exists, as the modern explicit recognition of the systematic ambiguity inherent in linguistic expressions grouped in terms of 'place' and 'time'. It is inherent as invariance with respect to groups of transformations. (Roughly, absolutely the same thing said or referred to in different ways.)

The point of this book is that 'God' and 'Science' disappear into choice between two or more courses of action, as *independence* of the direct object of knowledge and the indirect object of information. In other words, the *identity* of the two general meanings of 'object': something aimed at.

To formulate systematic ambiguity requires the use of modern symbolism, making explicit distinctions which are ignored in the vagueness of ordinary language, although lengthy discussion in the vernacular can induce conviction.

Hence the terseness of this book, which presupposes on the part of the reader some sophistication: sophistication not so much as technical background but rather as the grasping of complex relations through his or her having transcended a level of social organisation characterised by the bank's having taken the cathedral's place as centre of life.

One transcends it in *recognising* that quantitative comparison is possible only in terms of *the same* standard.

But of course to reach this self-realisation is not easy with a vanishing belief in only two possibilities.

'And God said'

The object of the holy name and the technical term can be said to exist *only* in the process of our recognising each other, as agreement to differ in the definition of expressions implicitly by the context – conditions necessary and sufficient.

INTRODUCTION

Science and God

By 'Science' here is meant the kind of determinism referred to by Charles Handy (R2, *The Hungry Spirit* 1997, p 80), determinism as the belief that what happens in the world happens in accordance with 'laws' which we can 'discover'. In other words statements of statistical uniformity are treated not as averages or primarily descriptions of facts but as rigid 'physical laws' or 'forces of nature'. Such mechanical determinism is found sometimes even in genetics. According to some people we are in every way predetermined by our inherited genes. An extreme form of this kind of scientific explanation postulates that all events including human actions are predetermined, and that it should eventually be possible to predict the course of any human's life moment by moment.

The late eighteenth-century French mathematician Laplace is best known for his belief in mechanical determinism. However his foundation of probability theory, upon consideration of combinations of 'equally possible' cases, suffered from logical circularity. It did so in the sense that the definition of probability measure involves what is often called 'equally likely' outcomes of an experiment, which presupposes the concept of probability. To quote M J Moroney:

The dictionary tells me that 'probable' means 'likely'. Further reference gives the not very helpful information that 'likely' means 'probable'. It is not always that we are so quickly made aware of circularity in our definitions. We might have had an extra step in our circle by bringing in the word 'chance', but to judge from the heated arguments of philosophers, no extension of vocabulary or ingenuity in definition ever seems to clear away all the difficulties attached to this perfectly common notion of probability [R3, p 4].

There is indeed a philosophical problem for anyone who does not accept that 'equally probable cases' is independent of the other axioms of 'a mathematical model of the body of empirical facts which constitute our data' [R1].

The problem is often characterised as that of the presuppositions and implications of 'freewill' as opposed to 'determinism'. For the theist the problem takes the form: if the doctrine of creation is true, then can this leave any room for human responsibility and choice?

On the other hand, for the thoroughgoing determinist, life could appear to be utterly meaningless, especially as mechanistic explanations had by the eighteenth century reduced God to a mere initial impulse leaving the Universe to its lawful devices once the process of creation had been completed.

However, empirical phenomena do not only take place. They are repeatable.

In the thirteenth century, St Thomas Aquinas, developing the traditional Aristotelian position in relation to Christianity, produced 'proofs' of the existence of God in which it was taken for granted that explanation was required not only for every initiation of change but also all continuations of it.

Also for Aquinas, man's freedom, far from being destroyed by his relationship to God through initial divine decree, finds its foundation in the very relationship to a creative Providence that wills each being to act according to its proper nature.

By the nineteenth century, in spite of the successes of a purely secular science (e.g. Darwin's), God could be conceived as revealing Himself through the external world or, on the other hand, believed in as majestic 'otherness' beyond the reach or apprehension of experience; but God is most popularly regarded traditionally as the creator in the sense of the great Designer.

In the following, 'God' means mainly the object as design or purposiveness in the Universe, whereas 'Science' refers to the view of objects as subjects of 'laws' as inflexible as clockwork.

In 1982 an advertisement on a London tube station wall, for a series of public introductory lectures on philosophy, started with 'Throughout the ages Man has asked simple yet fundamental questions. Who am I? What is the purpose and function of my life? What is my relationship to the world at large?'

This essay is concerned with the phenomenon of the quest for purpose or meaning shown by the contemporary proliferation of neo-religious cults and by the back-to-God writings of some professional scientists, as well as exhortations of bishops, politicians, educationists and journalists stressing the need for a return to 'standards' or traditional norms of behaviour in today's world of sleaze, crime, vandalism, drug taking and the general breakdown of traditional family values. For example, Archbishop Carey has condemned the flight from values as a 'privatised DIY morality' (*The*

Times, 28 August 1996) and stated that moral confusion has weakened society (*The Times*, 31 March 1997). Cardinal Hume too has called for a return to values that fulfil needs. Among lay advocates of returning to 'standards', the computer science professor David Gelernter has exhorted Americans to become 'judgmental' again, criticising a society 'too squeamish to call evil by its right name' (*The Times*, 20 September 1997).

Today's world is also a world of deadly serious 'sport', science fiction, charismatic cult gurus, 'Jesus Christ Super Star', rehashes of bits of the Christian religion mixed with bits of old Eastern religions, men going around with bare feet or a shaven head in search of the great secret – amid messages about Armageddon, salvation and the 'meaning of life'. The money-makers who, according to the newspapers, are so often behind the gurus, cults and big drive-in church systems could not make their money if there were not many people in today's world of declining orthodox religion who are troubled by doubt or uncertainty.

Time was, long ago, when people's personal problems were dealt with by father confessors of the Church in a religious context which gave meaning to so many aspects of people's lives. The way the wind has been blowing in recent times was shown for example some years ago by the very appearance in *Time* magazine of an article in effect asking: what if anything has religion to offer today? Yet sometimes even self-styled atheists refer to human beings as having been 'programmed'. Who is the programmer?

Even within the Church itself, the twentieth century has seen theologians claiming to be 'Christian atheists' and in Britain recently there have been new arguments about whether God exists. To quote the *Guardian* article 'Wide Eyed and Godless' of 4 September 1993: 'The debate about God is breaking out again, more seriously and more radically than in the sixties, when Bishop John Robinson of Woolwich liberated many would-be Christians from the straitjacket of a literalist belief in physical miracles. This time Christians – and priests at that – are saying that God does not exist (because nothing exists) outside human minds. And they still claim to be devout Christians'. And in the same article, of priests writing philosophically in the *Church Times*: '...to rid themselves and their congregations of the anachronistic encumbrances of the supernatural. These people find their new freedom exhilarating. Inspired by Don Cupitt, the Cambridge theologian whose TV series 'The Sea of Faith' popularised the non-realist view of God nine years ago... The debate continues'.

Under the changing conditions of modern life and social circumstances of individuals there have been many expressions of doubt or uncertainty regarding traditional values and beliefs:

> The increasing interest in revivalist and charismatic religions may be one response to the increasing uncertainty of the modern world. It is a search for another sort of certainty, one unconnected with the material universe [R2].

In this essay, it is contended that the 'solution' to the 'problem' is to be found in modern Science itself; but the 'solution' to such a general 'problem' is inevitably extremely abstract.

What is so striking is the contrast between the intuitively corporeal character of neo-religious utterances or aims and the very abstract nature of modern scientific theory.

The difficulty of an inevitably very analytic approach in trying to deal with questions such as those about meaning or purpose in life, or their lack, was succinctly expressed in the early part of this century by Bertrand Russell who opened his book *The Problems of Philosophy* with:

> Is there any knowledge in the world which is so certain that no reasonable man could doubt it? This question, which at first sight might not seem difficult, is really one of the most difficult that can be asked ... philosophy is merely the attempt to answer such ultimate questions, not carelessly and dogmatically, as we do in ordinary life and even in the sciences, but critically, after exploring all that makes such questions puzzling, and after realising all the vagueness and confusion that underlie our ordinary ideas. In daily life, we assume as certain many things which, on a closer scrutiny, are found to be so full of apparent contradictions that... [R4].

One kind of contradiction is the way in which contemporary expressions of concern about lack of purpose, in the Internet age, seem paradoxically to imply a surfeit of useless information. Moreover the neo-religious quest for meaning or purpose is echoed in many a newspaper article – in this modern world of statistics (i.e. bits of information for *processing*) – in spite of the widely acclaimed work of modern 'philosophers of Science' organising a variety of experiences by formally identifying explanatory theories on the basis of an ultimate uncertainty principle variously called the axiom of choice, the principle of duality or systematic ambiguity. In other words, absolute sameness in the sense that an axiomatic theory intended to formalise some intuitive theory is 'categorical' if different interpretations of the theory are indistinguishable apart from differences of terminology and notation; information processing thus being regarded as independent of limitations of place and time.

Such formal unifying structures could appear, aside from the difficulty of following the technicalities, to be general abstract nonsense having little relation to 'real life'. Hence the widespread attitude that science cannot resolve our feelings of confusion amid the contradictions of the modern world, in spite of its material benefits. (It is significant that Handy subtitled his book [R2] *Beyond Capitalism – A Quest for Purpose in the Modern World*.)

However, one can find the same abstract formal pattern in the real-life value theory given in Marx's *Capital* in which it is fundamental that in this world of commodities (a commodity being 'primarily ... a thing whose qualities enable it, in one way or another, to satisfy human wants') the generically human character of labour constitutes its specifically social character; and so the object is independent of the forms of human society, as conveyed by Marx's 'Urged to action by the need for clothing men made garments for thousands of years before anyone became a tailor'.

However, Marx's theory has been subject to a myriad of different interpretations ranging from those expressing economic determinism to those expressing historicism in the sense of 'laws of development' permitting long-term social forecasts.

In spite of Marx's apparently determinist and prophetic utterances and in spite of the apparent limitations of his 'labour' theory which he took over from Ricardo and other economists, Marxian value theory can be regarded as an interpretation of what is known as abstract group theory in the language of modern science, aiming definitively at uniqueness of reference. It is an *important* interpretation, for its initial objects are easily recognisable as relevant to our interests. It starts from the fact that we are constantly being put into situations where we must express a preference, must make a choice between two or more courses of action. Meaning is implicitly defined by the context, the dual 'object' being used by us to express a function. God as Ultimate Purpose and Science as merely deterministic disappear into this very distinction, between 'two or more' alternatives.

Noting the exchange-relation implied in the production of a commodity, an object able to satisfy human wants 'in one way or another', we begin the following chapters by showing in more detail how Marxian value theory can be regarded as an interpretation of abstract group theory.

References

1. Cramér, H (1946) *Mathematical Methods of Statistics*. New Jersey, Princeton UP.
2. Handy, Charles (1997) *The Hungry Spirit: Beyond Capitalism – A Quest for Purpose in the Modern World*. London, Hutchinson.
3. Moroney, M J (1956) *Facts from Figures*. London, Pelican.
4. Russell B (1912) *The Problems of Philosophy*. Oxford, Oxford University Press.

1

MARXIAN VALUE FORMS AND GROUP ELEMENTS

This chapter leads up to showing, in Chapter 2, how the value theory given in Marx's *Capital*, and to some extent in his *Contribution to the Critique of Political Economy* (rather than the apparently prophetic stuff of his propagandist or slogan writings) can be regarded as group theory.

It is concerned with Marx's theory as one example of the recognition of *reversal of order* of antithetical phases in a developmental process, shown in the writings of various nineteenth-century philosophers, scientists and sociologists. The period from the time of the industrial revolution was characterised by writers for whom, instead of a relatively spatial world in which all unfolds itself with complete determinism, the world unfolded temporally, in time. One has only to think of the strong historical or epochal sense of Hegel, Darwin, Lyell, Comte or J S Mill – to say nothing of the way in which the classical Greek 'self-evident truth' returned as the early nineteenth-century mathematicians' 'axiom', but regarded by them as a consciously adopted fundamental assumption – while in the arts romanticism similarly meant a return to medieval or earlier values.

In the same era, in science the direct method of

'induction', generalising from experience, was giving way to the indirect method, which makes use of deduction to test a hypothesis by inferring its consequences for testing in practice. In this way lesser generalisations are explained, in the sense of being connected into a theoretical system. Mere empirical generalisations are only descriptive. They are in need of explanation. An object or event is isolated until we can assign its 'cause' in an empirical 'law'; an empirical law is isolated until we can derive it from a wider generalisation. This derivation is accomplished by formulating, between the two generalisations, some element of identity conditioning the 'laws' of less generality, in the sense that properties of things belong to groups, one member of a group implying another member of the *same* group. The essential characteristic of the group is inversion of order of succession: each member has an inverse member with respect to the functional dependence rule of combination (the rule into which each member and its other disappear).

Cause

To grasp the significance of inversion of order (that is of revolution, literally) in a developmental process it is vital to understand the origin of 'cause' as some anthropomorphic Agency which *produces* its effect. It is easy to confuse knowledge with information, overlooking that the earliest use of language is to stimulate actions and evoke responses, not to communicate information or to indicate properties.

With the evolution of primitive man self-consciousness begins to emerge, as an affect which, though awakened by a stimulus, appears to lead a solitary life of its own.

The fear becomes the thing feared; the desire, the thing desired. Everything in the world seems to be alive. (So *we* say, *about* a primitive.)

The 'ultimate questions' referred to by Bertrand Russell, in *The Problems of Philosophy*, originally arise when, out of the immediacy of primitive animism the, more organised, pagan religious believer finds that his prayers are not always answered and then in turn leaves the 'contradictions' for philosophers to consider.

So to try to put in a nutshell what the so-called problem of philosophy is or has been by starting formally with the philosophies of ancient Greece, as is so often done, without making some reference to the animism of primitive societies and the religions of the ancient delta civilisations as well as those of Greece and Rome, for example the Pythagorean doctrine of immortality of the soul, would be futile.

Such an approach would amount to failure to recognise philosophising as an activity of people concerned with what is presupposed and implied by various kinds of discourse, and so rooted in the particular level of social organisation to which the philosopher concerned happened to belong.

First of all, in the magic rituals of primitive society an object begins to be distinguished from its fleeting appearances. A primitive does *not* of course say to himself: 'I am a member of a low-level social organisation, a tribe'. *We* say that he projects himself directly into external nature in the form of spirits (animism) and that his feeling of control is the actual control of things. To talk about a primitive or unsophisticated person is one thing, to be primitive or unsophisticated quite another.

Similarly, one indulges the behaviour of children,

aware that one has been a child oneself, without any longer being able to see things through a child's eyes.

A fundamental difficulty in trying to formulate problems inherent in one's life conditions or social circumstances is that the 'problems' arise as such only when the conditions for their 'solution' are *already* in process of formation.

In their relatively undeveloped social context, of signs 'significant by convention' (Aristotle) there was no 'problem' for the ancient Greeks in terms of what much later became Cartesian dualism between the mental and the physical.

From the time of the ancient Greeks up to nineteenth-century European civilisation the anthropomorphic or activity view of causation persisted, first of all as efficient or prior cause versus cause as an end, aim or purpose. The popular notion of cause is based on experiences such as a flame bursting out when one pokes the fire. The earliest stages of what we would call scientific investigation assumed the form of a *search* for causes, while the technical language of the sciences contained terms such as 'force' and 'energy'.

However, with the advance of science there was growing emphasis on the causal *relation*. For example, in the late seventeenth century, Locke wrote: 'A cause is that which makes any other thing ... begin to be, and an effect is that which had its beginning from some other thing' [R1, II, Ch XXVI] or, with less emphasis on the relation of *producing*, 'Put a piece of gold anywhere by itself, separate from the reach and influence of all other bodies, it will immediately lose all its colour and weight...' [RI, IV, Ch VI].

In the seventeenth and eighteenth centuries, while some philosophers regarded a causal relation as knowledge derived from actual experience of constant regularities, others were prone to searching for governing principles independent of experience which would enable us to say what kind of thing must have been responsible for the existence of the Universe or of human beings.

Whether emphasis was laid on the causal relation or on the terms of the relation, up to the nineteenth century the use of 'cause' was an oversimplification, presupposing isolation of one or more properties of events from a total set of *conditions*.

Causal connections are never found pure but are always associated with conditions which are 'irrelevant' to them. In the nineteenth century Mill laid stress on 'conditions'. He recognised that the distinction between cause and condition is often arbitrarily drawn:

> Nothing can better show the absence of any scientific ground for the distinction between the cause of a phenomenon and its conditions, than the capricious manner in which we select from among the conditions that which we choose to denominate the cause [R3].

A result of emphasis on a causal term instead of upon the relation was to stress unduly sharply the temporal priority of the cause to the effect as opposed to the spatial or continuity aspect of the relation. The emphasis on the relation itself resolved this ambiguity only by over-emphasising necessary conditions *vis-à-vis* sufficient conditions for an occurrence. Explanations thus tended to mere logical consistency without consistency in the wider sense, of completeness. So the ambiguity in the use of 'cause' as the selection of a striking or impressive factor out of the set of factors that are jointly sufficient and independently necessary to the production of the effect fails to recognise that what we have to take into account is a system the parts of which are in mutual dependence. The relation of causation ceases to be of importance, disappearing into the distinction between necessary and sufficient conditions; in other words the inversion of order expressed by the logicians' 'if and only if'. The expression 'p if and only if q' is an abbreviation for the joint assertion of 'if q then p' and 'if p then q'. It is important for the precision or uniqueness of reference characteristic of a science as it becomes what we call 'scientific', requiring exact definitions.

Bertrand Russell, in his essay *Mysticism and Logic* said that in advanced sciences such as gravitational astronomy, the word 'cause' never occurs, adding, 'the reason why physics has ceased to look for causes is that, in fact, there are no such things' [R4].

There certainly are no such things *now*.

The expression 'if and only if' rarely occurs in ordinary discourse but is employed widely in those abstract disciplines where precise definition is necessary.

Definition

With the development of the law/lawgiver ambiguity implicit in 'cause' there was bound up the progressive definition of scientific terms. The proposition/judgment ambiguity implicit in the subject-predicate relation of Aristotle, who had regarded the definition of a thing as expressing the characteristics it had to have to be the thing it was, led, by the fifteenth century, to the question: do we define names or what the names stand for? This disappears into the distinction between real and nominal definition.

For it is in the distinction, the relation itself, ultimately agreement as the same thing said in different ways, which is all important in Science aiming with the utmost abstraction at uniqueness of reference.

A definition is expressed in terms of *other* expressions that are taken as undefined and forming an analysis of the expression to be defined. In fact definition is pointless without the undefined term. Definition enables us to see what we were meaning when we *used* the expression that is now defined – meaning defined implicitly by the context rather than spelt out explicitly. We define an expression but there is an expression to define only because we want to talk about what it expresses.

The disappearance of the 'real' and 'nominal' objects in Marx's language

For Marx, use-value was 'realised only in use or consumption'. He was fundamentally concerned with the undefined term as inversion of order, as that which is independent of simultaneous transformation and substitution of the terms of an exchange relation – in the way that the terms of any simple equation are different and *yet* the same. In the case of the definition of expressions in common use the choice in the 'selection' of the undefined terms is never conscious; it results from the development of language under the pressure of practical needs.

However, as in the case of the undefined terms of the mathematical scientist's deductive system which is susceptible of various interpretations in the relating of different disciplines, Marx began *Capital* by referring to his 'commodity' inevitably from a high level of abstraction. Having introduced it as a thing whose qualities enable it, in one way or another, to satisfy human wants, he wrote:

> The nature of these wants, whether for instance they arise in the stomach or in the imagination, does not affect the matter. Nor are we here concerned with the question, how the thing satisfies human want, whether directly as a means of subsistence (that is to say an object of enjoyment) or indirectly as a means of production [R2, p 3].

That Marx was writing from the viewpoint of a high level of abstraction *about* particular concrete occasions of actual happenings which he had long since transcended, through the prevailing climate of opinion developed by his predecessors, made his work very difficult to follow for the less sophisticated reader.

From Marx's time up to the end of the 'cold war' between Eastern self-styled Marxists and the West, many of whose English speakers seemed to regard 'Marx' as a 'four letter word', much of the argument and discussion about Marx's theory, both by Marxists and non-Marxists, centred on what he called his 'guiding thread', a passage often quoted by other writers from his *Contribution to the Critique of Political Economy* of 1859. According to this passage the production relations of human beings which are 'definite and necessary' and are 'independent of their will' in the social production of their means of life, constitute:

> ...the real basis upon which a legal and political superstructure arises and to which definite forms of social consciousness correspond. The mode of production of the material means of life deter-

mines in general the social, political, and intellectual processes of life. It is not the consciousness of human beings which determine their existence, it is their social existence which determines their consciousness... At a certain stage of their development the material productive forces of society come into conflict with the existing production relationships. Or, what is a legal expression for the same thing, with the property relationships within which they have hitherto moved... A period of social revolution then begins...
[*A Contribution to the Critique of Political Economy*; Karl Marx; Eng. trans., Stone; pp. 11 ff.]

Marx's definite *and* necessary relations imply that what he called, elsewhere, antagonistic social 'classes' are defined by the 'real basis'.

The question arises: how are real basis and ideological superstructure related? Marx's work has been referred to as a two-storey house without a stairway. Moreover some writers have complained that Marx never clearly defined what he meant by 'class', although he held that since primitive times there had been two: one of which controls the means of production and the other which does not.

Marx's 'class' was not a collection in the sense of a mere set, but a group, a set whose members are defined mutually and reciprocally by functional differentiation; and Marx made clear in his 'guiding thread' that the form of the production relations is not that of an antagonism between individuals but one inherent in the life conditions and social circumstances of the individuals, at the time when the productive forces are creating the conditions for the solution of that antagonism.

By Marx's time the concept of 'class division' or the concept of 'class conflict' or 'class consciousness' was familiar to educated people. But up to the late eighteenth century, 'social class' meant primarily rank.

With the distinction between the class as order or rank and class defined as functionally social division, there is bound up the fact that Marx's theory as concisely expressed in the preface to the *Contribution to the Critique of Political Economy* has been subject to many different interpretations ranging from those expressing economic determinism to those stressing sociological historicism by their long-term prophecies or predictions.

Capital

However, the theory sketched in outline in his early works was presented more carefully by Marx in volume one of *Capital* (1867).

Marx, who saw his problem in *Capital* as discovering the origin and tracing the development of what he called the 'money form', started with commodities as use-values and then addressed their differentiation into exchange-values out of their appearance as merely qualitatively the same, already latent in barter.

In the first chapter, Marx outlined his value theory by means of three 'forms of value': (A) the 'elementary'; (B) the 'extended'; and (C) the 'generalised'.

The second chapter, concerned with the exchange of commodities by their owners and their latent differentiation of values, leads to the third chapter dealing with money as the means of exchange. The third chapter deals with the whole process of exchange from a purely formal point of view, being about the changes of form of commodities effectuating the social circulation of commodities.

In the fourth chapter this formal analysis is continued into discussing the transformation of mere money into capital.

Marx stated early in the book that the expression of value of 'commodities' represented by his 'elementary' form (20 yards of linen = 1 coat, representing accidental or occasional barter) was the 'germ' of the whole development with which he was concerned, adding that 'linen = coat is the groundwork of the equation'. One commodity, linen, actively expresses its value, in the coat.

In analysing his germinal equation fully he explained, in *Capital* how what he had called (in his *Contribution to the Critique of Political Economy*, 1859) the ideological superstructure 'reflects' what he had called the real basis. But many self-styled Marxists seem never to have read carefully Marx's writings apart from the first bit of the *Contribution to the Critique of Political Economy* and those incorporating 'slogans'. The result has been much argument about Marx's alleged 'materialism' or 'determinism'.

That Marx was not a crude determinist is shown in *Capital* in which he was fundamentally concerned with *choice*. In developing his theme he could only move from his 'germ' or 'elementary form' of value (and thence to the 'general equivalent') by invoking 'anyone you please'. The following passage sums up Marx's value theory:

> Any commodity you please to select may serve as mirror of the linen's value ... The labour which creates it is expressly represented to be labour which is essentially the same as all other human

labour, in whatever bodily form that labour may happen to be incorporated.
[R2, p 35].

In the elementary form the linen and coat, though qualitatively equated, play different roles. The 'value' (magnitude of value) of one commodity only, the linen, is expressed, by its relation to the coat as that for which it can be 'exchanged'. On the other hand only as value is the linen of equal value with the coat and exchangeable for it.

That which is *common* to different kinds of commodity in an expression of their equivalence is called by Marx 'abstract', 'undifferentiated' or 'homogeneous' human labour or the 'normal activity of human beings' [R2, p 16]. 'When the coat is equated with the linen the tailoring is in actual fact reduced to that which is identical in the two kinds of labour, is reduced to their common quality as human labour' [R2, p 21].

It is important to note the 'in actual fact', in connection with Marx's admittedly purely formal treatment of exchange, just as he wrote that in producers' exchanging:

> ...they equate the different kinds of labour expended in production, treating them as homogeneous human labour. They do not know that they are doing this, but they do it. Value does not wear an explanatory label. Far from it, value changes all labour products into social hieroglyphs. Subsequently, people try to decipher these hieroglyphs, to solve the riddle of their own social product [R2, p 47].

In the exchange of products of different kinds, the

'different kinds' are indicated by the *order* of the terms of the equation, read → or ← (though the different kinds are the 'same' as terms of the *equation*).

Marx's theory was characterised fundamentally by bivalence (two possible values in the sense of 'take it or leave it'). In his second chapter, about exchange, he stated that it is an essential part of the nature of all commodities, that they are not use-values for their owner, and that they are use-values for those who do not own them. 'The first step by which a useful object is enabled to become an exchange-value is that it should have an existence which has not a use-value for its owner' [R2, p 62].

Having distinguished at the beginning of *Capital* between the use-value and exchange-value 'factors' of a commodity, use-value being 'only realised in use or consumption' and exchange-value showing itself 'primarily as the quantitative ratio in which use-values of one kind are exchanged for use-values of another kind', Marx wrote (in the section headed 'The form of Value or Exchange Value'):

> Commodities come into the world as use-values, such as iron, linen, wheat, etc. This is their straightforward natural form. They are, however, commodities only in virtue of their twofold character, simultaneously as useful objects and as depositories of value. Consequently, they can only manifest themselves as commodities, or can only have the form of commodities, in so far as they have a twofold form; a bodily form and a value form [R2, p 17].

Use-value and exchange-value are both called 'value'. One might even say that the point of the theory is that definition is pointless without the undefined term. Marx wrote in his *Theses on Feuerbach* that the philosophers have only interpreted the world in various ways, the point, however, being to change it. He obviously knew what he was doing in his own admittedly formal treatment of exchange of products.

The equation, or first form of value

In a key section of *Capital* [R2, p 18], Marx distinguishes two value forms in which a commodity can present itself: 'relative value form' and 'equivalent form', as the 'polar opposites' of the 'elementary, isolated or accidental form of value' (the first form). In this germinal equation a commodity (A) is in the 'relative value form' solely by expressing its value by means of a contraposed different commodity (B) which figures as an equivalent; the 'equivalent form' meaning that (B) is directly exchangeable for (A). 'In so far as a commodity A expresses its value in the use-value of another commodity B, it stamps on the latter a peculiar form of value, that of the equivalent'. On the other hand the bodily form of (B) serves 'as mirror to the value of the commodity A'. (A and B are linen and coat in the concrete instance above.) Here we begin to recognise the ideological or superstructural 'reflection' which appeared in the preface to the *Contribution to the Critique of Political Economy*. (A) plays an 'active' role and (B) a 'passive' one in the elementary expression of value. But in one and the same expression of value 'one commodity cannot simultaneously appear in both forms'. The elementary form of value is the initial form of a system of levels of abstraction in the sense of 'degrees of development' in the 'developmental relation' [R2, p 40] between the 'relative form of value' and the 'equivalent form'; first of all in the 'total or extended form of value' which is Marx's second form, of which form the 'extended relative form of value' and the 'particular equivalent form' are polar opposites. (Marx had already remarked, about the first form or 'germ', that (A) and (B) are reciprocally dependent factors; but at the same time mutually exclusive extremes.)

The second form

Regarding the developmental step to the second form it is to be noted, as remarked above regarding choice, that Marx wrote that the elementary form, in which the value of a commodity is expressed in terms of only one other commodity, passes 'of its own accord' into the more highly developed or extended form, in which 'any commodity you please to select' may serve as mirror to the value of any one commodity, for example linen.

The whole 'mystery' which 'lies hidden' in Marx's elementary form is that of *order*. Accordingly as we read the elementary equation forwards or backwards, each of the two commodity poles will function 'alternatively and indifferently' in the relative and equivalent forms. But in the second form of value this polar contrast begins to become clear:

> In the second form, only one kind of commodity can fully extend or develop its relative form of value; and it only acquires this extended relative form of value because, and in so far as, all other commodities function, in relation to it, as equivalents [R2, p 40].

In the second form, the magnitude of value of a commodity is 'more effectively distinguished from its own use-value': for in the expression of value of any one commodity 'all other commodities appear only in the form of equivalents'.

Marx's 'extended relative form of value' consists only of a series of relative expressions of value, or equations of the first kind, such as:

20 yards of linen = 1 coat
20 yards of linen = 10 lbs of tea, etc.

Though 'human labour has its complete phenomenal form...' in the totality of these particular phenomenal forms this 'does not give it a unitary phenomenal form' (Marx had already remarked about the second form that it was defective, as an endless series of expressions of value 'mirrored' in fragmentary equivalent forms). Inverting the equations gives his 'generalised form of value'. (It is to be noted that this step to the third form refers to the fact that choice is made between alternatives – to the 'at the same time' reciprocally dependent and mutually exclusive factors.)

The third form of value

$$\left. \begin{array}{l} 1 \text{ coat} = \\ 10 \text{ lbs of tea} = \\ \tfrac{1}{2} \text{ ton of iron} = \\ 1 \text{ qr. of wheat} = \\ 4 \text{ lbs of coffee} = \\ \text{etc.} = \end{array} \right\} 20 \text{ yards of linen}$$

'The third form ... gives to commodities at large a

generalised social relative form of value because, and in so far as, all commodities save one are excluded from the general equivalent form. This means that one commodity ... has acquired the character of being directly exchangeable for all other commodities ... because, and in so far as, other commodities have not acquired that character ... , [R2, p 41]. As linen equivalent, the value of each commodity is distinguished, 'not only from its own use-value, but from all use-value', and 'by that very fact' its value is expressed as something which it has in common with all commodities. By the third form commodities are for the first time made to confront one another *as* exchange-values. A commodity cannot acquire a generalised expression of its value unless all commodities simultaneously express their values in the same equivalent. All commodities now appear not only as qualitatively the same, not only as values in the general sense of the term, but also as quantitatively comparable magnitudes of value.

However, when Marx stated that each of the equations of the second form 'implies' its reverse and 'Let us, then, invert the series' to get the generalised form of value; also that 'A commodity cannot acquire a generalised expression of its value unless all commodities simultaneously express their value in the same equivalent, so that every new commodity has to follow suit', he was anticipating his purely formal treatment of the 'whole' exchange process. For his theory deals with the circularity implicit in exchange, the paradox recognised by a set-theorist as that of the set of all sets which are members of themselves.

That choice between alternatives is *postulated* is remarked by Marx in a footnote on his page 41:

It is far from being self-evident that this character

of being generally and directly exchangeable is, so to say, a polar one, and is as inseparable from its polar opposite, the character of not being directly exchangeable, as the positive pole of a magnet is from the negative.

In Chapter III of *Capital* this reappears in the form of the use/exchange value inseparability, as ordinary commodity and the money commodity, from the antithesis of sale and purchase.

Change of form of a commodity in exchange

In his Chapter III Marx assumes that gold (not linen) functions as the money commodity, so that the expression of the value of a commodity in gold, x commodity A = y money commodity, is its money form or its *price*.

The equation need no longer figure as a link in a chain of equations. The price of commodities is, like their form of value generally, distinct from their palpable and real bodily form. The value of iron, linen, wheat, etc. though it is invisible is made ideally perceptible through a relation to gold.

In so far as the process of exchange transfers commodities from a person for whom they are not use-values to a person for whom they are use-values the product of one kind of useful labour replaces the product of another kind. As soon as it has reached the spot where it can serve as a use-value the commodity falls out of the sphere of exchange into that of consumption. This leads Marx to consider exchange purely from the point of view of the changes of form of commodities which bring about their social circulation.

'Every change of form in a commodity results from the exchange of two commodities one for another, one of them being an ordinary commodity and the other the money commodity'. Marx emphasised the role of the commodity owner using gold as a means of exchange: 'If we confine our attention to the material fact that a commodity has been exchanged for gold, we overlook the very thing we ought to see, namely what has happened to the form of the commodity. We overlook the fact that gold as a pure commodity is not money, and that when other commodities express their prices in gold, this gold is but the commodities themselves in a new metamorphosis, in the money form' [R2, p 81].

Marx gives an example. A weaver exchanges 20 yards of linen for £2, then exchanges his £2 for a family bible priced at the same figure. The process of exchanging commodities is completed in two opposed and complementary metamorphoses: the transformation of a commodity into money, and the retransformation of the money into a commodity. The two phases of this metamorphosis are both of them *effected by the owner* of the commodity. The two transactions have a unitary character, that of selling in order to buy.

The result of the whole process as regards the weaver is that instead of having the linen commodity he now has another commodity of the same value but having a different utility.

The exchange of commodities is effected by means of the following changes of form:

Commodity   –   Money   –   Commodity
    C   M   C

The result of the whole process is, so far as concerns

the objects themselves, C–C, the exchange of one commodity for another.

When the result is achieved, the process is at an end. Marx considered in some detail the various aspects of the two phases of the complete metamorphosis of a commodity: C–M (sale) then M–C (purchase).

As regards *sale*, the first partial metamorphosis, the linen's price of £2 has already brought the linen into relation with gold as money. The shedding of the original commodity form occurs at the moment when its use-value actually attracts the gold that previously had a merely ideal existence in its price. The realisation of the price is therefore at the same time the realisation of the ideal use-value of money. The first metamorphosis is a sale from the outlook of the commodity owner. From the outlook of the money owner it is a purchase. In other words C–M is also M–C.

Moreover, apart from the exchange of gold for commodities at the source of production of gold, in whoever's hands it may be gold is the transformed shape of some commodity as the product of a sale. We cannot tell from looking at a particular piece of money for what particular commodity it has been exchanged. This consideration leads Marx to expand his example, assuming that the two gold pieces for which the weaver has exchanged his linen are metamorphoses of a quarter of wheat. The sale of the linen is the first act of a process that ends with a transformation of an opposite kind, the purchase of a bible. On the other hand the purchase of the linen ends a movement which began with the sale of a quarter of wheat:

    C–M   (linen – money) which is the first phase of
    C–M–C (linen – money – bible) is also
    M–C   (money – linen), the last phase of

C–M–C (wheat – money – linen)
(First metamorphosis of one commodity is simultaneously the second and opposite of another.)

While on the one hand money represents a sold commodity, on the other, it represents purchasable commodities. M–C, *purchase*, the concluding metamorphosis of the commodity, is at the same time C–M, a sale. The last metamorphosis of one commodity is simultaneously the first metamorphosis of another commodity. So Marx further expands his example, assuming that the bible seller spends the £2, received from the weaver, upon brandy:

M–C (money – bible) the concluding phase of
C–M–C (linen – money – bible) is also
C–M (bible – money) the first phase of
C–M–C (bible – money – brandy)

However, since the realised price is split up for numerous different purchases, the final metamorphosis of a commodity is an aggregation of the initial metamorphoses of various other commodities. The *complete metamorphosis* of a commodity presupposes, in its simplest form, four extremes and three contracting parties, one of whom intervenes twice:

> First of all, the commodity is confronted by money as its value form, by the money which, in another person's pocket, has concrete reality. The owner of the commodity is, therefore, confronted by an owner of money. As soon as the commodity has been transformed into money, this money becomes its temporary equivalent form, whose use-value or content, for its part, exists in the

bodies of other commodities. Money, as the goal of the first transformation, is at the same time the starting-point of the second. Thus the person who is seller in the first act, becomes buyer in the second, when a third owner of commodities confronts him as a seller [R2, p 89].

The circulation of commodities differs from •the direct exchange of products, known as barter, in substance as well as in form:

> The weaver has certainly exchanged his linen for a bible, has exchanged his own commodity for a commodity that belonged to someone else. But this phenomenon is only true for him. The seller of the bible, who has a taste for something that will warm up the cockles of his heart, had no thought of exchanging his bible for linen, any more than the weaver knew that wheat was being exchanged for his linen. B's commodity replaces A's commodity, but A and B do not reciprocally exchange their commodities [R2, p 90].

There develops a multiplicity of social relations that are 'spontaneous in their growth and are quite outside the control of the actors. The weaver is only able to sell his linen because the farmer has sold the wheat; the bible agent is only able to sell the bible because the weaver has sold linen; the distiller is only able to sell the strong waters because the bible agent has already sold the waters of eternal life; and so on' [R2, p 91].

We see here one aspect of the conditions 'independent of their will' mentioned in the preface to the *Contribution to the Critique of Political Economy*. The other aspect (of 'definite and necessary') is referred to by Marx's 'Consequently, the process of circulation does not, like direct barter, come to an end as soon as the use-values change places or change hands.'

Money does not disappear but is constantly being precipitated into new places vacated by other commodities. When one commodity replaces another, the money commodity always remains in the hands of some third person.

Transformation of money into capital

Marx started Chapter IV of *Capital* by stating that the circulation of commodities is the starting-point of capital.

He had remarked in Chapter III that purchase and sale are one and the same action when regarded as a mutual relation between two persons who are polar opposites, the owner of commodities and the owner of money; but that purchase and sale are themselves polar opposites regarded as the actions of one and the same person.

The first metamorphosis of the linen brings coins into the weaver's pocket, the second metamorphosis takes them out again. From the *weaver's point of view* the two changes of place of the coins, movements in opposite directions, form a spatial relation. But as seller he retains the power of going into circulation at any *time* once he has sold in order to buy thus completing the metamorphosis of his commodity – before acting *again*. There is the *possibility* of the duality inherent in a commodity, as value and yet use-value, becoming explicit.

Marx wrote that the primary distinction between money as money and money as capital is nothing more than a difference between their respective forms of circulation:

The simplest form of the circulation of commodities is C–M–C, the transformation of a commodity into money, and the retransformation of money into a commodity, selling in order to buy. However, side by side with this form we find another, which is specifically different. We find the form M–C–M, the transformation of money into commodities and the retransformation of commodities into money, buying in order to sell. Money that circulates in this way is thereby transformed into capital [R2, p 132].

Regarding the circuit M–C–M, it is stated in *Capital* that this circuit would be absurd and unnecessary were it to eventuate, after all our trouble, in nothing more than the replacement of a certain sum of money by exactly the same amount.

The only way in which one sum of money can be distinguished from another is in respect of magnitude. This leads Marx to calling 'surplus value' the increment or excess of the final value over the original value [R2, p 136].

Marx then grapples with the paradox of how one must buy commodities at their value and sell them again at their value, and nevertheless at the end of the process draw more value out of circulation than one puts in at starting.

What distinguishes 'the form which circulation takes when money becomes capital ... from the simple circulation of commodities is the inverted order of succession' of the two phases, sale and purchase. 'How can this purely formal distinction change, as if by magic, the nature of these processes?' [R2, p 141].

Marx concludes that the change must take place in the commodity bought by the first act M–C; not in the value of that commodity, seeing that equivalents are exchanged. 'Consequently the change cannot arise anywhere except in the use-value of the commodity, in its consumption...'. This leads to a 'commodity whose use-value has the peculiar quality of being a source of value, a commodity whose actual consumption is a process whereby labour is embodied, and whereby therefore value is created..., labour power or capacity for labour' [R2, p 154].

In this sense Marx is back where he started, abstract human labour.

To an old-fashioned or unsophisticated logician, circularity in an argument is something terrible. Of course, in the relatively restricted contexts of everyday arguments a circular argument is normally rejected. However, if the context is so extended as to become so general as to amount formally to definition in use, circularity in the sense of the postulational method itself is inevitable.

The general formula of capital makes its appearance within the sphere of circulation, going back on itself to use-value 'realised only in use'.

In C–M–C the same coin changes places twice. The seller receives it from the buyer, and pays it away to another seller. In M–C–M, what changes place twice is the same commodity. The buyer receives it from the seller and passes it on to another buyer. Just as the twofold changes of place of the same coin bring about its definitive transference from the hands of one person into the hands of another, so the twofold changes of place of the same commodity effect the return of the money to its starting point.

The simple circulation of commodities is a means for the satisfaction of wants; but the circulation of money as capital is an end in itself – for the expansion of value can only occur within this perpetually renewed movement, so the circulation of capital is endless.

It is as the *conscious representative* of this movement that the owner of money becomes a capitalist.

We recognise here the 'superstructural' reflection of the 'real' basis in the preface to the *Contribution to the Critique of Political Economy*. We also recognise the distinction between money's two different functions referred to in Marx's second and third chapters of *Capital*: money as means of exchange as the 'social incarnation of human labour', and money as unit of account as the 'standard of price'.

In the circuit M–C–M commodity and money serve only as different modes of existence of value. Value is 'the active factor in a process, in which, while continually assuming by turns the form of money and the form of commodities, it at the same time changes in magnitude, gives birth to surplus value, so that the original value spontaneously expands' [R2, p 140]. (Note the 'by turns' for our next chapter in which the mutual exclusion and reciprocal dependence functions are symbolised geometrically and counter-clockwise.)

In simple circulation the value of commodities acquires nothing more than the independent form of money as confronting their use values. But in the circulation of capital this same value distinguishes itself as its primary value from itself as surplus-value, 'much as God the Father distinguishes himself from himself as God the Son', yet both in fact forming one person. (When Marx's weaver re-sells his linen the inversion of order, of sale and purchase, exists for him alone.)

The distinction here, between God the Father and God the Son, the distinction between utterly abstract knowledge and concretely mediated information – the distinction into which they both disappear – is the same as Marx's 'simultaneously' or 'at the same time' or 'any commodity you please to select'; or the set theorists' distinction between set-membership and set-inclusion. As Marx wrote, the value of a commodity is distinguished not only from its own use-value but from all use-value; and by that very fact its value is expressed as something which it has in common with all commodities. In other words he was concerned with the group identity element, between generality and singularity.

References

1. Locke, J (1690) *Essay on the Human Understanding.* Everyman, 1976.
2. Marx, K (1930) *Capital,* London, Dent. English edition. Introduction by G D H Cole.
3. Mill, J S (1843) *System of Logic.* Collected Works, Routledge, 1996.
4. Russell, B (1953) *Mysticism and Logic, and Other Essays.* Harmondsworth, Penguin.

2

BETWEEN THE DETERMINED AND THE UNDETERMINED

In this chapter, Marx's farmer-weaver-bible agent-distiller example will be represented geometrically in order to symbolise the serial relation generating an order of repetitions in patterns.

The relation is independent of the interpretation of the symbols used in the process of analysis, in that the series is *distinguished* from the elements exhibiting serial order. Marx's value theory is used here for this purely formal treatment of exchange because abstract mathematical logic could appear to have little to do with real life, whereas Marx's language is about objects whose properties enable them to satisfy human wants in various ways. So Marx's value theory, in which use-value is defined only in use or consumption, is translated into the statement in which it is asserted abstractly that possession of one property is a necessary and sufficient condition for possession of another. *In other words* it forms a group.

A group is a system composed of a set of elements a, b, c and a rule for combining any two of them to form their 'product' such that:

(1) every product of two elements is an element of the set;
(2) the associative law (ab)c = a(bc) holds;
(3) the set contains an identity element 'I' such that Ia = aI = a for every element; and
(4) each element a has an inverse a^{-1} such that $aa^{-1} = a^{-1}a = I$.

If the elements of the group are just abstract symbols which have no interpretation except as elements of the group, the group is called an abstract group.

In an assignment of meaning to the otherwise undefined terms of the system, Marx's value theory is recognised as *an* interpretation of the abstract group.

Marx's farmer, weaver, bible agent and distiller are represented *respectively* by the vertices A, D, B, C of a tetrahedron, shown in Figure 2.1.

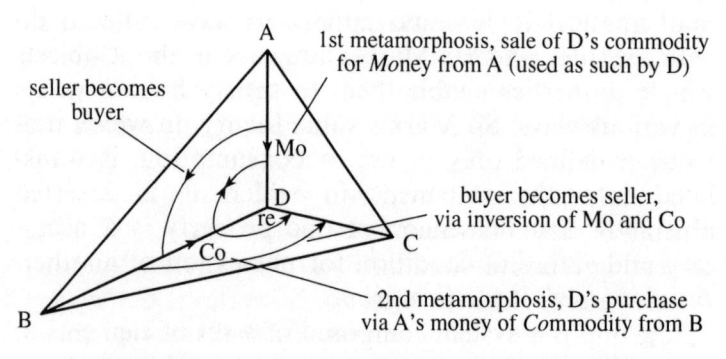

D's commodity exchanged for B's as result (re) of D's and B's each selling in order to buy.
Money *returns* to D, from C as result (⋈) of D's (in use of B) buying in order to sell.
(B and D simultaneously express their values through *A* in selling to D, C respectively; but this is *recognised by D alone*)

Figure 2.1

They form a system of parts which are in mutual dependence, B being functionally dependent on D as elementary seller, and so on. B and D simultaneously express their values through A, in selling to D and C; but the order inversion is *recognised by D alone*. *Circulation* splits up the identity of direct exchange into the antithesis of sale and purchase in accordance with the associative rule of combination 'between': if D is between A and B and B is between D and C, then B is also between *A* and C. The rule is associative in that it asserts that it is immaterial how the parentheses are inserted in $(AB)C = A(BC)$, 'between' implying separation of pairs (B is not only distinguished from A but also from any one other than A, D by means of B thus pairing A *and* C).

In communicating to B something which B does not know, D functions as a (singular) name for at least one other, B. However, in B's repeating D's information (the way in which D's sense-data is interpreted) in turn for C, D's knowledge (what *D* knows) is represented as a (general) name for any one other than A. Thus D and B know something in common, the identity element forming, as it were, the context in which the communication occurs.

As *independence* of insertion of parentheses, the associative rule is a trinity.

Treating the inverse elements DA and DB as 'points' of a projective 'line' turning about vertex D, also BD and BC as 'points' of a projective 'line' turning about vertex B, these 'lines' are 'parallel' having no 'points' in common. In consequence, the change of form $A\overline{DB}$ and the change of form BDC which are formally the same unit, as *ordered pairs*, from D's viewpoint, can be treated as equal 'alternate angles' of the 'points' DB and BD which socially (by D's metrical parameter

A → B) constitute a 'transversal', their common 'line' from A to C (the 'segment' attributing C to A as *recognised by D alone*) of the 'parallels'.

The identity of giving and taking in direct exchange is not a self-evident truth, but a fundamental *postulate*, for in the nineteenth century the 'axiom' of parallels was shown – by *renaming terms* of ordinary Euclidean geometry – to be *independent* of the other axioms of Euclidean geometry.

Long after Euclid, during the period when pure Euclidean geometry (the main distinguishing feature of which is, in one or other equivalent form, the postulation of the equality of alternate angles of a transversal of parallels) gave way to the reference axes of 'coordinate' geometry (in which the linear/angular duality has become explicit), doubts arose about Euclid's postulate and eventually mathematicians felt that it should be capable of being proved. The Greeks had not been worried by what their successors eventually called the 'parallel postulate'. This expression was introduced after it had been found that every proof presented was fallacious, usually by begging the question in some way. After Playfair's formulation, at the end of the eighteenth century, of the parallel postulate *as* a postulate, attempts to prove it gave way, in the nineteenth century, to non-Euclidean geometry. With the advent of non-Euclidean geometry, in which the parallel postulate was replaced by a contrary postulate amounting to the extension of 'Euclidean' to a more abstract space (that of the 'projective plane' of a vertex or the 'metrical parameter' of a segment), the question whether it was possible to prove the parallel postulate was settled, negatively. The advent of non-Euclidean geometry dispelled the belief that the parallel postulate could be derived from Euclid's remaining axioms. The independence of the parallel postulate was shown by constructing a system whose consistency was established by renaming terms of Euclidean geometry so as to give a 'model' of the non-Euclidean system, as a linguistic translation of the system into ordinary Euclidean geometry.

This was of considerable significance, as it represented the entertainment of the possibility of varying the meaning of the otherwise undefined terms of an explanatory theory while retaining its deductive structure. In this way Marx's value theory can be regarded as another interpretation of abstract group theory.

Arithmetic

Also in the nineteenth century, the independence of the parallel postulate was mirrored in the metrical aspect of geometry by Kummer's showing that under the assumption of unique-prime factorisation (pairing) 'Fermat's Last Theorem' could be proved [R1]. He showed it in linguistic translation, by *renaming* elements of classical Greek arithmetic thus recognising unique prime factorisation. (In modern mathematics unique prime factorisation is 'restored' in ideal number theory, of additive and multiplicative ideals [R2]).

The question of unique prime factorisation became prominent after Kummer's work on 'Fermat's Last Theorem' which states that for $n > 2$ the equation $\chi^n + y^n = z^n$ cannot be satisfied by positive integers χ, y, z (of course it holds for squares and $n = 1$).

Fermat in the seventeenth century had claimed to have devised a proof of what became known as 'Fermat's Last Theorem', a proof of which he stated he could not reveal 'because there is not enough room in the margin' of the paper on which he was writing. Fermat, who did much of his mathematics longhand, was probably not bemused by manipulation of symbols. Perhaps he had an inkling of the fundamental assumption implicit in the ancient Greek arithmetic which he studied, an assumption only made explicit after his time.

What the geometrical and arithmetic postulates have in common is consciousness – pairing as the identity in recursive definition. As the social act or systematic ambiguity of our definitions in one-to-one correspondence (as in the binary scale of notation) definition is normal. For the normative distinction ('if and only if') tending to establish a standard of correctness statistically, by prescription of rules chosen 'between' two or more courses of action, enables one to recognise oneself as the standard. Reflected in others one needs another. (D is the conscious member of the pair $\{B, D\}$ – see Figure 2.2.)

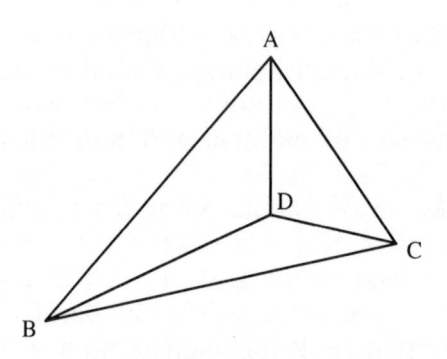

Figure 2.2

A and B do not reciprocally communicate, but 'there develops a multiplicity of social relations' independent of the 'control of the actors' – independent of limitations of space and time – in the way that in the abstract group the identity element is invariant with respect to transformations and translations.

The logical and aesthetic norms are inverses with respect to the ethical norm. Mere information of direct knowledge, though dead, lives on in the inherited culture of society.

Lineal *and* multiplicative it is ideal.

References

1. Bosevich, Z I & Shafarevich, I R (1966) *Number Theory* (trans.). New York, Academic Press.
2. Northcott, D G (1953) *Ideal Theory*. Cambridge, Cambridge University Press.

The Two Aspects (active and passive) of
'The turning point of all history'
(Simone de Beauvoir)

3

THE SAME THING SAID IN DIFFERENT WORDS

The ambiguity of 'is' as predicative or existential is systematic in that it can be formulated according to a rule in the sense of recursive definition of terms.

Systematic ambiguity

In explicitly recognising *the same* unit or identity element, the standard presupposed in all quantitative comparison – the 'multiplicity' of social relations which are 'quite outside' the 'definite and necessary relations' into which human beings enter in the production of their means of life – Marx foreshadowed the modern independence of the explanatory on axiomatic theory, independence of *other* presuppositions, those of sampling. For each datum is collected, data being taken as a *whole* in processing them. In interpreting quantitative data a 'statistic' can mean a bit of information or an average of bits, something singular or general and so the meanings of 'statistics' are not sharply separable in *individual* recognition of them.

However, the first clear signs of such recognition can be found in the *Analytics* of Aristotle, to whom Marx referred as 'the great thinker who was the first to analyse so many of the forms of thought, society and nature' [R4, p 30]. Marx's general approach, the systematic ambiguity of terms as singular or general names, was recognisably the same as that of Aristotle. As indicated below at length, the approach is formally the same as that of the identity element of a grouping system, involving a 'first cause'.

Aristotle's First Cause argument was an explanation not only of every initiation of change but of all continuations of it.

This led on the one hand, through the empirical generalisations of Renaissance experimental science, to the Forms of Science as mechanical determinism; and on the other hand, through the medieval schoolmen who constructed Christian theology on the basis of Aristotle's works, to God as Providence.

As governing repeatable empirical phenomena, Providence was at bottom the statistical norm, identity or standard.

However, in their relatively undeveloped social context, the context of symbols as signs 'significant by convention' (Aristotle), classical and medieval logicians were not able to regard agreement to differ as fundamentally definition of meaning implicitly by the context. The rigid 'law' was not yet a mere statistical uniformity recognised as such. Admittedly the term 'induction' which is often supposed to characterise scientific method originated with a word introduced by Aristotle, although the early use of the term to refer to generalisations from particular instances or to enumeration of instances was so unclear that it has been used very ambiguously by subsequent writers apparently unaware of ambiguity as systematic, in one's taking datum and data as a whole.

On account of his *classifications* and generalisations Aristotle is often regarded as the first scientist. Perhaps that was why Bertrand Russell omitted him from the series of all the major philosophers, from Plato to Hegel, mentioned in his book *The Problems of Philosophy*. On the other hand, as there was yet no 'problem' of dualism for the classical Greeks, Aristotle was also a theologian in his teleological, 'Final Cause', view of the Forms, which he had inherited from Plato who in turn had been influenced by the Pythagorean doctrine of immortality of the soul.

However, in his astronomical writings Aristotle did seem to recognise to some extent the independence of cause as effective/final, in his regarding the heaven as a sphere because a sphere is the perfect figure; it rotates in a circle because only circular motion, having no beginning and no end, is 'eternal' – which can be interpreted statistically as the *present*, completely independent of limitations of space and time (time-measure being datum-data).

It is, in other words, the mathematical ideal governing repeatable empirical phenomena, as the circularity of alternate base and remainder in the arithmetic binary scale of notation; also as that of the trinity of the undefined term 'between' ordering the revelatory sign and agreed symbol as polar opposite extremes in definition of terms. It is also recognisable as the ideal of choice between extremes in Aristotle's *Ethics*.

Systematic ambiguity, the otherwise undefined term of contextual definition, formulated recursively according to a rule of definition in use, was foreshadowed in Aristotle's principle of the syllogism: 'Whatever is said of the predicate is said of the subject'. We all know the abstract relation 'between' as transitive by pairs, between 'alternatives'. Aristotle's principle as applicable to a related case or group of cases is applicable to propositions stating relations between attributes: 'An attribute of an attribute is an attribute of the subject'. So it takes the form of the traditional categorical syllogism.

Syllogistic reasoning

Syllogism is a form of reasoning in which from two given or assumed propositions, called the premisses, and having a common or middle term, a third is deduced called the conclusion from which the middle term is excluded.

The traditional categorical syllogism is of the form:

              M as such is P
              S is M
Therefore   S is P

Aristotle called the subject and predicate of the conclusion the 'extreme' terms. They may be represented by the letters S and P respectively.

The term M which mediates the conclusion in connecting the extremes has been *traditionally* called the 'middle term'. Aristotle named the predicate of the conclusion the 'major' term and the subject of the conclusion the 'minor' term. The premiss containing the major term is called the 'major' premiss, that containing the minor term is called the 'minor' premiss. So it is impossible to determine which is the major premiss and which the minor without (recursively) referring to the conclusion.

The ancient Greeks distinguished four 'figures' of the syllogism, figure being the form of a syllogism as determined by the function of the middle term in the two premisses. If account be taken of the premisses alone, only three figures are possible:

1	2	3
M–P	P–M	M–P
S–M	S–M	M–S
∴ S–P	∴ S–P	∴ S–P

For M must be either (1) subject in one premiss and predicate in the other, (2) predicate in both, or (3) subject in both.

The arrangement of terms in the premisses of each figure necessitates our filling in the blank between the terms with 'is' or 'is not', or their plurals, and prefixing the signs of quantity, 'some' or 'all'. An example, in figure 1, is:

All men are fallible;
Some advisers are men;
So some advisers are fallible.

The Following example, in the second figure, was given in Aristotle's *Ethics*:

All truly moral acts are done from a right motive;
Some acts which benefit others are not done from such a motive;
Therefore some acts which benefit others are not truly moral.

If, however, it is determined which term shall be the subject, and which the predicate, of the conclusion, the distinction between major and minor is introduced into the premisses and a fourth figure is possible, distinguished by depending not on the order of the two premisses but on the position of the middle term in the respective premisses:

$$\begin{array}{c} 4 \\ P\text{--}M \\ M\text{--}S \\ \therefore S\text{--}P \end{array}$$

Aristotle, who devised a method for reducing syllogisms in figures 2 and 3 to figure 1, regarded the fourth figure as a useless variety of the first. An example of this figure would be:

Moderate exercise is beneficial to health;
Everything beneficial to health is in accordance with medical advice;
So something in accordance with medical advice is moderate exercise.

Most arguments expressed in the awkward fourth figure would be more naturally expressed in one of the other figures.

The difference between the figure

$$\begin{array}{c} M\text{--}P \\ S\text{--}M \\ \therefore S\text{--}P \end{array}$$

and the figure

$$\begin{array}{c} P\text{--}M \\ M\text{--}S \\ \therefore S\text{--}P \end{array}$$

where again the premisses are written in the order of the major first, depends on observing the distinction between minor and major premisses. If these were transposed in the fourth figure, the figure would become:

$$M-S$$
$$P-M$$
$$\therefore P-S$$

In this case the major term is S and the minor P.

However, Aristotle's dictum 'Whatever is said of the predicate is said of the subject' involves an inversion of order of terms.

In his fundamental figure

$$M-P$$
$$S-M$$
$$\therefore S-P$$

between the premisses the role of M is switched from predicate in the minor premiss to subject of the major premiss, a switch from a functional to a structural role. In one's distinguishing between the minor and major premisses, as depending on the *position* of the middle term in the *respective* premisses, the *substitution* between the premisses results in a *statement* for any one other of an ordered pair of terms. When Aristotle rejected the analytic fourth form, he seems not to have recognised his own First Cause as also the cause of all continuations of change. (See Figure 3.1).

According to the traditional Aristotelian logicians, *whatever* is predicated of M is predicated of *any*thing that can be asserted to be a predicate of M. At the same time there is inversion of order, of S–P to P–S, between two different positions; so that the act of substitution is independent of spatial and temporal conditions, as a relation of exchange between transpositions of terms, in the *sense* of a group identity element, I.

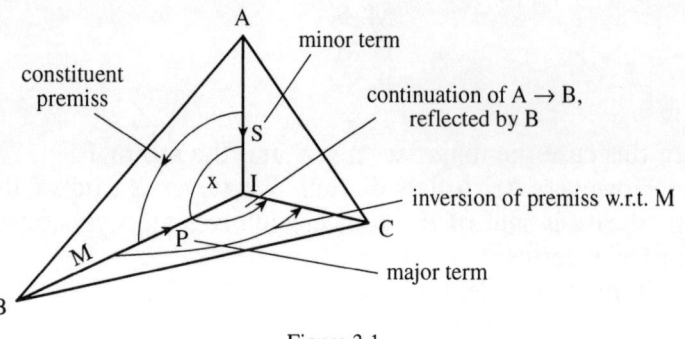

Figure 3.1

(labels in figure: A — minor term; constituent premiss; continuation of A → B, reflected by B; inversion of premiss w.r.t. M; major term; B, M, P, C, S, I, x)

Intermediate between figures 1 and 4, in figures 2 and 3, there is implicit spatio-temporal reference. In figure 3 the middle term of at least one proposition is chosen to function as subject of a conclusion, M being in the subject position; whereas in figure 2 the middle term of each proposition functions as an other-than-the one chosen, M being in the predicate position. So figures 3 and 2 differ as the singular and the general proposition – they differ as the process and the result (proposition/statement) of immediate inference, by which the implications of a single proposition are unfolded (see Figure 3.2).

Just as the S–M premiss is an ordered pair in I's sense of bringing about a change of place, so the *consequent* M–P premiss brings about a reversal of order, a reversal for I alone.

The premisses of the classical syllogism are 'propositions'. According to the Aristotelian tradition, a proposition is anything that is believed, disbelieved, doubted or supposed. For Aristotle not every 'sentence' is a proposition, only such propositions as 'have in

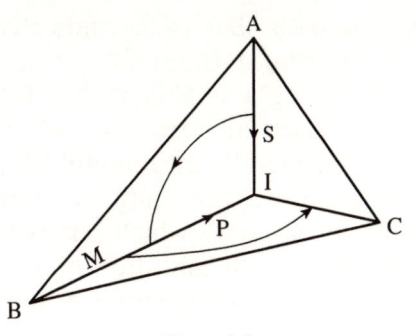

Figure 3.2

them truth or falsity', only those sentences which express what is either true or false. (So that prayers, commands and exclamatory sentences are not propositions.)

However the intermediate figures 3 and 2 are implicitly dual involving the distinction between I's direct knowledge and I's information incompletely enumerative of the subject.

But the distinction of the fourth from the first figure does not depend on the *order* of the two premisses but on the position of the middle term in the major and minor premisses respectively. In I's reversal of S → P the conclusion is a *statement*, completely enumerative of S.

In modern times 'proposition' and 'statement' have been used in various ways, some text-book writers regarding a statement as something whose fundamental property is to be true or false; and what some logicians call the statement calculus others call the propositional calculus. This does not lead to confusion in symbolic logic but as still hieroglyphically sacred the statement of a *proposition* is philosophically significant.

A J Ayer proposed that every indicative sentence, whether it is literally meaningful or not, shall be regarded as expressing a statement, but that the word 'proposition' be reserved for what is expressed by sentences which are literally meaningful [R1, p 8].

Certainly a statement is meaningless (not limited) in the absence of any response which serves to define the terms of a proposition. Substitution of symbols is not sharply separable from transposition of terms. Philosophical (sign/symbol) conundrums arise as soon as the immediate 'now' distinction between the life or death temporal elements ('one' or 'other') of a single propositional relation begins to be spatialised.

For I, the development of information is only the process and result of the development of knowledge. The 'as soon as' duality, of proposition-statement (3-2) formulated in terms of the syllogistic figures 1 to 4 can be formulated in terms of truth-tables.

Truth-tables

In various text-books of logic and switching-circuit design a truth-table is a scheme of rows and columns for exhibiting the *conditions* under which a truth functional connective, for example 'or' or a connecting wire in a 'parallel' combination, is T or F. In the table each row represents a possible combination of the two truth-values for the component propositions of the compound, there being sufficient rows to cover all possible combinations.

Thus, assuming that every proposition is either true or false, there are only two possibilities to consider for the connective 'not' and the simple one-place table for *negation* ($\sim \chi$) of the proposition χ is:

χ	$\sim\chi$
T	F
F	T

The syllogism as determined by the changed role of the middle term is invariant with respect to simultaneous interchange of S and P and of major and minor premisses – just as the truth-table:

χ	y
T	F
F	T

customarily determining the truth function y as the negation ($\sim\chi$) of an argument, χ, χ and y being so related that exactly one is 'true' and the other 'false', is unchanged if T and F and also χ and y are simultaneously interchanged. Just as the distinction between minor and major premisses depends on observing the position of the middle term in the respective premisses of the syllogism, so the distinction between a proposition and its negation depends on whether one starts with value T in the left hand column or in the right hand column. (Thus one has another case of interchanging ordered pairs.)

Connectives

In:

χ	y	(i)
T	F	
F	T	

as representing mutually exclusive values of one and the same variable, one truth value of the two possibilities {T,F} is chosen (T) to function as a singular name (χ) for at least one alternative, other than the one chosen. So a singular name determines a proposition according to the table:

χ	y	for at least one of {χ, y}
T	T	T
T	F	T (ii)
F	T	T
F	F	F

Moreover as represented by reciprocally dependent values each of χ and y is not only distinguished from its own T value but brought into relation by T as a common name ($\sim \sim$) for *any* one other. So a general name, or property, defines a statement according to the table:

χ	y	for any one of {χ, y}
T	T	T
T	F	F (iii)
F	T	F
F	F	F

(The dual connectives 'for at least one' and 'for any one' are formally the same as the text-book tables for the connectives ∨, 'or', and ∧, 'and'; often symbolised in terms of 0 and 1 instead of F and T.)

However, 'any one' is functionally dependent on 'at least one' as the substitution of one truth value for the other of 'at least one'. So substituting the values opposite to those in the χ column of (ii) (exactly as in the text-book composite table for '∼ χ or y') there is obtained, after some algebraic manipulation, a table explicitly defining a statement as representing another:

χ	y	y dependent on χ (if χ then y)	
T	T	T	
T	F	T	(iv)
F	T	F	
F	F	T	

In other words, a T-statement implies a T-statement consistently.

'If and only if'

But as χ and y are reciprocally dependent statements of the general name or defining property, substituting the 'if χ then y' and 'if y then χ' values for χ and y, taken in turn in the table (iii) (exactly as the text-book substitutions in the table for 'and') we obtain, after some algebraic manipulation, the table:

χ	y	'χ if and only if y'	
T	T	T	
T	F	F	(v)
F	T	F	
F	F	T	

where it is *agreed* that 'χ if and only if y' means 'if χ then y *and* if y then χ'.

The characteristic of the table is that if χ and y have the same truth value, then 'χ if and only if y' is true; if χ and y have opposite truth values then it is false.

So the characteristic is, expressed 'circularly', that 'χ if and only if y' is T if and only if χ and y have *the same* value. It is 'about' (i) in expressing that T is as inseparable from F as a general from a singular name. In other words, the assertion that a proposition's taking one value is a necessary and sufficient condition for the taking of another.

Although the expression 'if and only if' is not used in ordinary everyday language, it occurs frequently in disciplines in which precise definition is required. The 'and' of 'if and only if' is the language formation rule according to which there is formulation of systematic ambiguity – the 'one another' of words used in different senses yet in each case the usage is significant.

In other words it is ultimate circularity as the recursive definition, in terms of singular and general names, of the undefined term lost in the immediacy of primitive qualities defined only in use or consumption. It is regained, out of the (religious) substitution of a revelatory sign for the direct object of knowledge and the (scientific) substitution of an agreed symbol for the indirect object of information (with all their original sin 'tree of knowledge' which-is-which? problems) – by a procedure which is formally *the same* as that of the digit/place one-to-one correspondence positional notation of arithmetic or that of the column names in the truth-table defining negation, or the pattern of repetitions (see Figure 3.3).

This is mirrored in the principle of the syllogism, as shown in Figure 3.4.

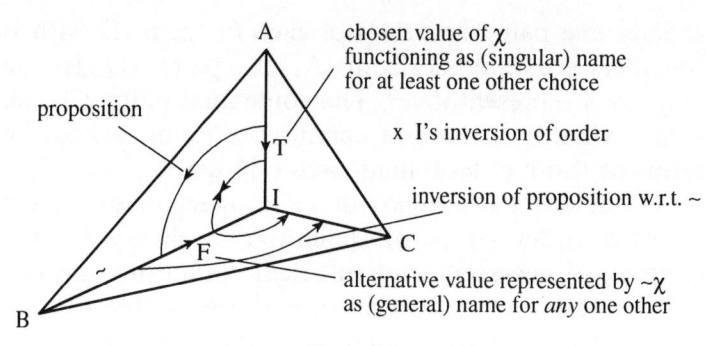

Figure 3.3

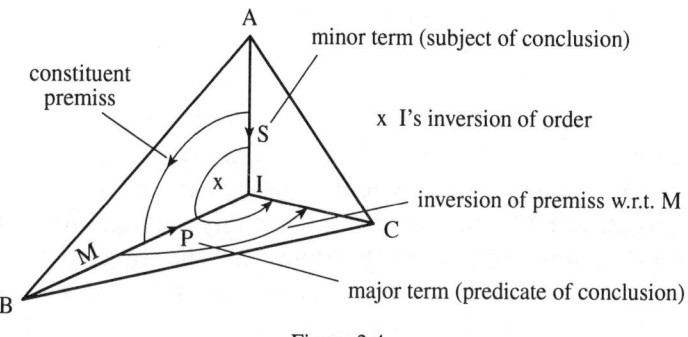

- proposition
- A: chosen value of χ functioning as (singular) name for at least one other choice
- x I's inversion of order
- inversion of proposition w.r.t. ~
- alternative value represented by $\sim\chi$ as (general) name for *any* one other

Figure 3.4

- constituent premiss
- A: minor term (subject of conclusion)
- x I's inversion of order
- inversion of premiss w.r.t. M
- major term (predicate of conclusion)

'Determination is negation' (Spinoza)

What the categorical syllogism and negation have in common with Marx's series-generating relation (symbolised as the parallel postulate in Chapter 2) is choice between alternatives: given an ordered pair of ordered pairs there exists an ordered pair consisting of exactly one pair (the *other*) of each of them (D with B together separate C from A, its pair) (D is the conscious representative). The contextual pattern is the same, whether in Marx's commodity terms, syllogistic terms or those of switching-circuit design.

As choice between two or *more* alternatives, in the inverted order sense of definition implicitly by the context, of necessary and sufficient conditions (instead of the merely philosophical opposition of freewill and determinism or Chance and Fate) the common formal pattern is independent as the identity relation presupposed by a partial ordering relation generating a series. It is independent of the simultaneous interchange of truth and falsity and of specific and general names, as the relation mirroring the endless series generated by 'between' in the separation-of-couples series, which is endless as *returning*.

In the definition of meaning implicitly by the context (rather than just *spelled* out *definitely*) religion and merely deterministic Science disappear in individual recognition of one another as socially related through 'fact', something already done. In the inversion of order I (D) becomes fully aware of the necessity of choice made in direct action. By I others are agreed to differ, made to confront one another as statements.

The identity relation can be *said* to exist only in the process of one's defining its terms, the *unordered pair* being presented as an ordered pair in which we are able to indicate every time only an other (see Appendix A).

Necessary and sufficient conditions

The identity relation 'exists' only in the sense of conditions which are sufficient and necessary. It is independence as choice between two or more courses of action, independence of differences of terminology and notation as the ultimate ambiguity of our definitions in one to one correspondence (the 'equivalence/relation').

In acting to satisfy immanent needs, that which is needed becomes the realised properties of objects; although it is religious enlightenment as the process of extending that which is holy. As referring to a unique object the differential or singular term is the aesthetic ideal.

On the other hand as the general term the socially necessary is realised as the logical 'law'.

But as necessary *and* sufficient the condition is the ethical norm or standard, the whole of which the other norms are parts, oneself (see Appendix B).

The trouble with narrow selfishness is that it is not selfish enough, failure to realise that self-realisation is possible only through one another. Definition by the context, of necessary *and* sufficient conditions, takes into account a system the parts of which are mutual dependence. Stephen Hawking has quoted Wittgenstein [R3, p 175] as saying that the sole remaining task for philosophy is the analysis of language. Hawking added 'What a comedown from the great tradition of philosophy from Aristotle to Kant!'

One notes the implicit existential and positivist aspects – 'remaining task' – of that which is 'sole'.

Philosophy has been a centuries-old struggle with the Aristotelian tradition, of the natural sign of originally pagan religion (see Appendix C) versus the conventional symbol originating in classical technology. The outcome of the struggle is agreement to differ in the sense of the ethical norm or probabilistic model governing repeatable empirical phenomena. After the time of Kant's categorical imperative – 'Act only on that maxim through which you can at the same time will that it should become a universal law' – there was a comedown for philosophy: it started to become explicitly sociological. Kant's 'at the same time' gave to the standard of behaviour a purely formal character, the character namely of being *the same* for all persons similarly conditioned. Since his time there has been growing recognition that the earliest use of language is to stimulate actions and evoke responses in independence of limitations of place and time, those of indicating properties and communicating information.

The old 'inductive logic' of 'scientific method' has given way to explanatory theory as that of statistical interpretation. The so-called begging-the-question fallacy in deduction, that of 'circular' argument from assumed propositions containing a common element, and the 'problem' of the validity of inductive inference, that of justifying the belief that what happens happens in accordance with 'laws', in arguing from observations to conclusions, have in modern times given way to the theory of statistical uniformities as datum *and* data. Probability theory, that of processes involving *uncertainty*, involves any way of getting a number describing the result of a trial or experiment, in other words *any* means of assigning meaning to the undefined terms of an axiomatic theory, thus specifying the theory.

The symbols O and 1 as used in probability theory for the absolute bounds of the ratio involved in the usual definition of probability measure – 'success' or 'failure' of a trial and its outcome – are formally reflected in the F and T of affirmation and negation, and the truth-tables for the singular and general names are reflected in the addition and multiplication rules of 'total' and 'compound' probability. The systems reflecting each other are indistinguishable apart from differences of notation and terminology.

One can only deal with form. The normal probability distribution is built up theoretically, on the assumption that the 'successes' or 'failures' that constitute the total occur at random or as 'equally likely'.

The uncertainty principle is bound up with the 'concept' of simultaneity as choice between alternatives symbolised by D's and B's separation of C from A, recognised by D (see Figure 3.5).

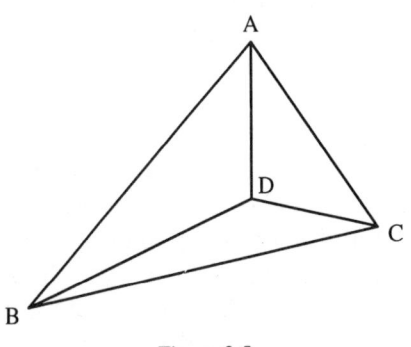

Figure 3.5

Of Einstein, who rejected the concept of absolute simultaneity on the grounds that all definitions of the simultaneity of events are relative to the frame of reference of the observer, Stephen Hawking wrote 'general relativity is a "classical" theory; that is it does not incorporate the uncertainty principle...' [R3, p 156].

In the nineteenth century, Marx, in spite of his own value theory, had similarly revealed a classically 'religious' rigidity or 'scientific' socialism with which was bound up the prophetic stuff in the '*Communist Manifesto*'; or bound up with the 'In my view' of the following quotation from his preface to the second edition of *Capital*:

> My own dialectical method is not only fundamentally different from the Hegelian dialectical method, but is its direct opposite. For Hegel, the thought process (which he actually transforms into an independent subject, giving to it the name of 'idea') is the creator of the real; and for him the real is only the outward manifestation of the idea. In my view, on the other hand, the ideal is nothing other than the material when it has been transposed and translated inside the human head [R4, p 873].

The 'In my view...' is still philosophical, dualistic, in spite of Marx's frequent 'at the same time'. Where is the probabilistic model of data processing?

With the simultaneous interchange of values and probability rules, in which just two chance opposites disappear in recursive definition of one another 'one is free of philosophical conundrums in realising that an average and the particular instance are as inseparable as the positive from the negative pole of a magnet' [R2, p 135] (or as inseparable as inertial/gravitational mass).

The variously expressed distinction between things future and things past is inseparable from their mutual dependence as revelatory signs and agreed symbols.

In short, ultimate ambiguity (see Appendix D).

References

1. Ayer, A J (1949) *Language, Truth and Logic*. London, Gollanz Ltd.

2. Gibson, R O (1995) *Freedom of Philosophical Conundrums*. Lewes, Book Guild.
3. Hawking S (1993) *A Brief History of Time*. London, Transworld.
4. Marx K (1930) *Capital*, vol. 2. London, Dent, English edition.

APPENDIX A

The independence of the religious and scientific 'object'

Although Marx wrote *Capital* in as 'popular a strain as possible' the very abstract nature of his value theory was necessary for broadly outlining 'progressive epochs in the economic formation of society' since primitive times, when the mythology and ritual of magic started to become religion and Science.

In this book Marx's theory has been represented in terms suggested by the nineteenth- and twentieth-century developments of mathematics which originated with the classical Greeks out of the rule-of-thumb mensuration and the digital grouping numerals of the pagan religious organisation of the ancient delta civilisations and the techniques of the ancient Ionians.

Classical Greek geometry systematised, in terms of intuitive 'self evident truths', the merely empirical generalisations of ancient civilisations even whose god-kings' prayers could not prevail against deterministic Fate or Law.

However, the Greeks' 'definitions', 'axioms' or 'postulates' could deal only approximately with questions involving the discontinuity of the line segment in contrast with the continuity of the angular vertex (bound up with the definition or simultaneity of sets of objects as limitations of place and of time) as in for example the determination of π.

Their methods were seen as only approximate from the points of view of their successors, particularly the sophisticated mathematicians of industrialised nineteenth-century Western society. With hindsight, the latters' axioms were consciously adopted assumptions instead of the classical Greeks' self-evident truths.

In the context of projective and differential geometry on the one hand and of algebraic and transcendental number theory on the other hand, nineteenth-century mathematicians developed theories of the abstract order of 'points on a line', theories which involved discriminating the relation 'between' from that of 'separation of couples'. This led to questions which could not be decided on the basis of axioms and to the question of the existence of the 'uncountable set'.

According to some influential modern mathematicians it cannot be said to exist, but that its elements only come into existence in the process of our defining them, the set being presented as a set in which we are able to indicate every time only a countable subset.

The relations involved as necessary and sufficient conditions in Marx's forms of value are here symbolised in mathematical terms in the way that the 'set' itself without elements is independent of assignments of place-holding variables and time-keeping functions to otherwise undefined terms.

APPENDIX B

The paradox of the religious norm represented secularly

In Marx's preface to the first German edition of *Capital* he wrote that the human mind had been vainly trying to fathom the *value form* for more than two thousand years.

In Bernard Shaw's play *Major Barbara* one character sarcastically retorts to another, who had claimed to know the difference between right and wrong, that the latter had solved a problem which had 'puzzled all the philosophers, baffled all the lawyers, muddled all the men of business, and ruined most of the artists'.

As regards philosophers: some have tried to show formally by pure logic that moral utterances merely express the reactions of the speaker – in what is nevertheless a psychological theory of value. On the other hand it seems that Nietzschean psychological criticism of man's need for religious belief was really an anticipation that the *übermensch* beyond Good and Evil would become a purely statistical norm.

In the endlessly self-correcting world of data processing by means of computers it is not easy for philosophers to recognise the standard of correctness in the *context* of mutual exclusion and reciprocal dependence – the Trinity's two aspects (compare chapter 2).

It is a striking paradox of contemporary Western culture – judging for example by the annual evasive sermons on the persons of the Trinity or by the enormous number of newspaper and other articles by authors worried that mankind is at a crucial stage of value-neutral development – that it is difficult to understand the value form as *at once* taking-apart and bringing together. As Bertrand Russell found, sets can be members of themselves.

The standard of correctness is the conscious representative of a perpetually renewed series constantly returning to its starting point as something already done, a 'fact'. It is the serial relation generating an order of terms in one-to-one correspondence or systematic ambiguity – free from the imperative set and from the indicative member of the Lawgiver.

APPENDIX C

The religious and scientific aspects of definition in use

What Marx called the ordinary and money commodities in his historical development of exchange are here distinguished as singular and general names in definition. Like Marx's 'any commodity you please to select', in this book it is assumed as absolutely fundamental that knowledge starts from choice made in direct action; but this implies separation, in that attention is drawn to one of many possibilities in the *naming* of which the object of choice is lost.

In order that D should communicate something to B, D must know something that B does not know; but in communicating information to B, D begins to distinguish an act of choosing from the object of choice, the choice then being made through another person.

The singular name is a sign, religious in the sense of a hieroglyph or 'sacred carving'. It is really religious, as belonging to the perceptual level of abstraction basic to the higher theo-*logical* level of abstraction characterised by the symbol.

By means of B's repeating information in turn for C, D distinguishes an act of choosing not only from its own object of choice but from every possible object of choice, thus generalising the singular name. The general name is a symbol, a 'throwing together', secondhand in the sense of an alphabetic ordering relation. It is ideally scientific as belonging to the *con*ceptual level of abstraction through which persons are socially related to the object.

Because the sign is rooted in similar behaviour it becomes the means, via the symbol, of organising social behaviour in reference to the *undefined term* presupposed in definition. The dead live on, really and ideally, in the inherited culture of society, as the interpretation of information.

APPENDIX D

For G Cantor the founder of set theory, which is so important in modern physical and social science, a set was any collection of definite, distinguishable objects of our intuition or of our intellect to be conceived *as a whole*.

The whole is ultimate as phenomenal/multiplicity.

The primitive terms – means and end – of an assertion or statement of fact are taken to be undefined.

APPENDIX D